BOY SCOUTS OF AMERICA
MERIT BADGE SERIES

SCHOLARSHIP

"Enhancing our youths' competitive edge through merit badges"

Requirements

1. Do ONE of the following:
   a. Show that you have had an average grade of B or higher (80 percent or higher) for one term or semester.
   b. Show that for one term or semester you have improved your school grades over the previous period.
2. Do TWO of the following:
   a. Make a list of educational places located where you live (other than schools). Visit one, and report on how you used the place for self-education.
   b. With your counselor's and your parent's approval, interview two professionals (other than teachers or other professionals at your school) with established careers. Find out where they were educated, what training they received, and how their education and training have helped prepare them for the career they have chosen. Find out how they continue to educate themselves. Discuss what you find out with your counselor.
   c. Using a daily planner, show your counselor how you keep track of assignments and activities, and discuss how you manage your time.
   d. Discuss the advantages and disadvantages of the different methods of research available to you for school assignments, such as the library, books and periodicals, and the Internet.

35946
ISBN 978-0-8395-3384-9

2013 Printing

3. Get a note from the principal* of your school (or another school official named by the principal) that states that during the past year your behavior, leadership, and service have been satisfactory.
4. Do ONE of the following:
   a. Show that you have taken part in an extracurricular school activity, and discuss with your counselor the benefits of participation and what you learned about the importance of teamwork.
   b. Discuss your participation in a school project during the past semester where you were a part of a team. Tell about the positive contributions you made to the team and the project.
5. Do ONE of the following:
   a. Write a report of 250 to 300 words about how the education you receive in school will be of value to you in the future and how you will continue to educate yourself in the future.
   b. Write a report of 250 to 300 words about two careers that interest you and how specific classes and good scholarship in general will help you achieve your career goals.

*If you are home-schooled or your school environment does not include a principal, you may obtain a note from a counterpart such as your parent.

Contents

School and You

How do you feel about yourself as a student? How do you see yourself in this important role? By the time you graduate from high school, you will have spent more than 2,000 days of your life in classrooms, accumulating more than 17,000 hours of instruction.

That's a lot of time and effort to put into the pursuit of knowledge. Believe it or not, how you perceive yourself as a student and how your teachers and school administrators see you, can make or break your academic experience. It might sound too simple to be true, but having a positive attitude toward your education is the single most important quality you can bring to your academic career.

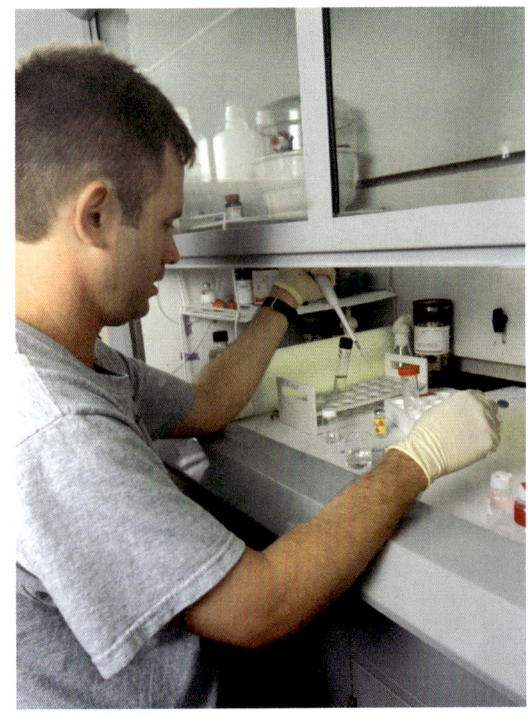

Why should an upbeat attitude toward school matter so much? Think about how hard it is to do something when your mind and heart aren't in it. It does not matter whether you are tackling a math problem or a football player on the playing field, if you are not interested in doing it, you probably will not give your best effort to achieve success.

Working on the Scholarship merit badge provides you with a great opportunity to become more successful in school. You will learn how to improve your skills in the classroom, develop good study habits, and master techniques for writing reports and taking tests. You will learn about the value of teamwork and how crucial it is that people appreciate each other's differences and work together effectively to achieve the best possible results.

Education provides the foundation from which you can reach your goals. No doubt about it!

A good, well-rounded education takes effort to achieve. Yet, your school days will fly by if you embrace learning as an exciting path of self-discovery and adventure. The more you learn about yourself and the world around you, the more opportunities will be available to you.

Surgeon General David Satcher

Dr. David Satcher, America's first African American male surgeon general (1998–2002), almost died from a double whammy of whooping cough and pneumonia when he was 2 years old.

But the young boy who lived with his family on a remote Alabama farm lived through the ordeal, thanks to an African American doctor who journeyed to the isolated Satcher homestead on his day off and stayed until the toddler was out of danger. He never forgot that experience. From then on, Satcher became increasingly interested in medicine and health. In 1998, President Clinton selected Satcher to serve a four-year term as the 16th surgeon general of the United States.

As America's doctor, he wanted to be known as the surgeon general who listened to the American people and who responded with effective programs. His mission was to make public health work for everyone, particularly with regard to proper health care, prevention programs, and treatment for all citizens. In particular, Dr. Satcher investigated how infant mortality, HIV/AIDS, diabetes, and cancer affect minorities and rural and urban populations.

He graduated from Morehouse College in Atlanta in 1963 and earned his M.D. and Ph.D. from Case Western Reserve University in 1970. He has served as a faculty member at the UCLA School of Medicine and Public Health. From 1993 to1998, he was director of the Centers for Disease Control and Prevention and administrator of the Agency for Toxic Substances and Disease Registry. He now serves as director of the National Center for Primary Care at Morehouse School of Medicine.

Not only does Dr. Satcher promote healthy lifestyles across the country as part of his work, but he also is an avid jogger and tennis player in his private life.

Esophagus
Squeezes food into the stomach
Stomach
Small Intestine

The Genuine Value of School

The basic knowledge and skills you gain in school can be applied toward job training and understanding other people better, and can offer unlimited opportunities for personal development.

The core subjects you are taught in school—reading, mathematics, writing, science, and social studies—form the foundation from which you will build your future. Reading and writing well, understanding and working math problems, and having a broad knowledge of history and how the physical world works, is vital to your ability to contribute to the society in which you live.

For example, say you dread English class because you have to write essays. Right now, you might not make the connection between how being able to write an essay will help you later in life, or how that scholastic skill is used in the real world. When you apply to college, however, you may be asked to write an essay on a specific subject. Particularly when a college receives many applications from students with excellent grades, school administrators lean heavily toward the best-written student essays to determine who will be accepted. Many scholarship applications also require an essay.

The elective classes you choose enhance your understanding of core subjects. Art, music, drafting, and a host of other electives enhance your overall education.

For job interviews, you might be asked to write a business letter or a short essay to demonstrate your ability to communicate. Learning how to write an effective letter now can pay off later when you look for employment.

Some of the math you learn might not seem useful, but as an adult, you will use math skills every day to balance your checkbook, estimate percentages for taxes and tips, and when you take measurements for any kind of building, home improvement, or hobby project.

In addition to building basic knowledge and skills, you will learn in school how to study effectively, how to plan and organize your schedule, how to research something that interests you, and how to analyze intelligently what you read in newspapers and see on television. When your school days are behind you, you will use the skills you learned in school to learn new things. You might not remember all the facts you memorized for tests, but you will never forget the skills you used to learn them.

One tool you might learn is called mind mapping. The trick is to boil down a complex set of information into a few sketches or pictures and/or as few words as you can use to describe the event.

Remember This

Beloved children's author Dr. Seuss, whose real name was Theodor Seuss Geisel, doodled a lot in school. His boyhood home still shows the marks of where he doodled on his bedroom walls. His teachers, for the most part, did not understand his need to draw, and he frequently got in trouble for daydreaming and sketching during class.

Although educators in his time did not recognize it as such, Geisel's doodling was a learning tool. Today, many teachers and schools teach students that drawing diagrams is an excellent way to memorize difficult and complex subject matter, such as historical information. Educators call this tool mind mapping, or using graphic organizers. Ted Geisel had no idea how this childhood "tool" would shape his future.

In college, Geisel started to draw cartoons for the student newspaper. Afterward, he wrote a children's book that made learning English fun. Geisel shopped the book around to nearly 30 publishers, but everyone thought it was too far-out, too goofy to take seriously. Eventually, one publisher saw Geisel's genius and the rest is history. Dr. Seuss became the world's top-selling author of children's books.

Suppose you are studying U.S. history and you need to remember a sequence of events that led up to a particular result. For instance, let's say you are studying the forced removal of the Cherokee tribe from their ancestral homelands in Tennessee, North Carolina, and northern Georgia to the newly created Indian Territory (Oklahoma) on the Trail of Tears in 1838–39.

Your teacher states that the following factors led to the Trail of Tears: Gold was discovered on Cherokee lands in Georgia in 1828, the Indian Removal Act was passed by

Congress in 1830, the U.S. Army forcibly took Cherokee lands for settlement, and evicted Cherokee were imprisoned in military stockades in early 1838. You would write down each of these events in a circle and/or make simple drawings within each circle to help you remember each event leading to a circle titled "Trail of Tears, 1838–39."

Your drawings and circles of information might look something like the following.

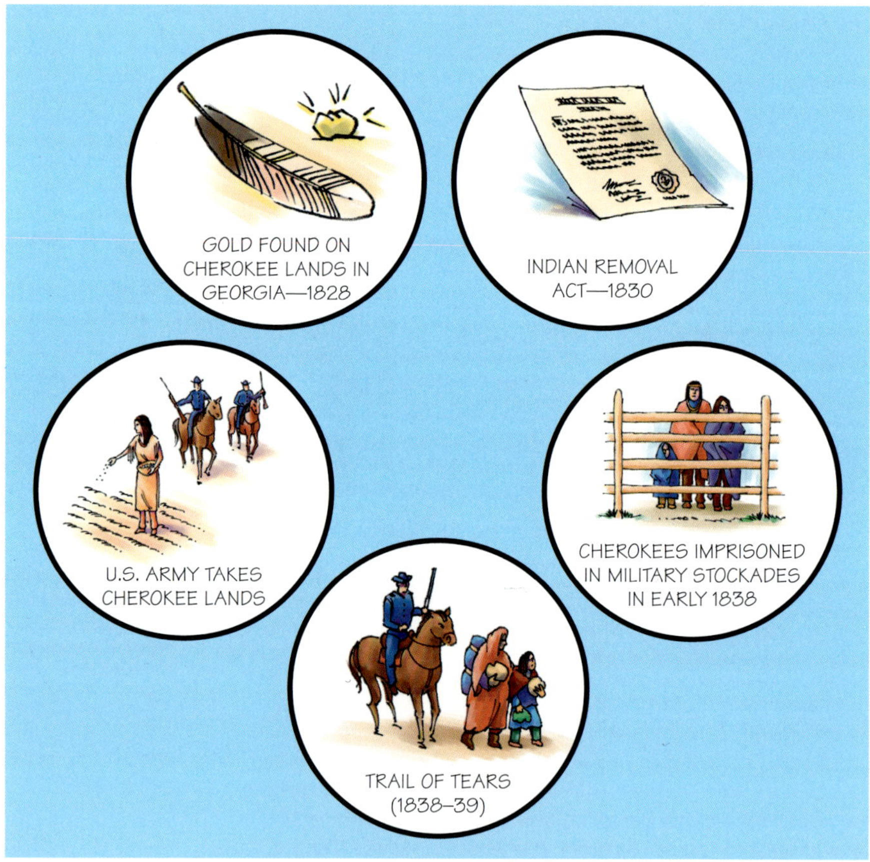

These simple sketches might not mean much to anyone else, but having a visual image you created to go along with the material you are learning will help you recall the information later.

Let's say the information you need to mind map is not sequential information; that is, the information is not a sequence of events that led to a particular result, but rather, it is a variety of factors that combined to create a new situation. For instance, let's say you are studying Great Britain's motives for colonizing North America. You would write the topic in a center circle. In circles surrounding the center circle, you would write or draw the motives. Then you would draw lines from each circle to the center circle, like the spokes of a wheel. All circles lead to the center circle.

A diagram of Great Britain's motives for colonizing North America might look like the following.

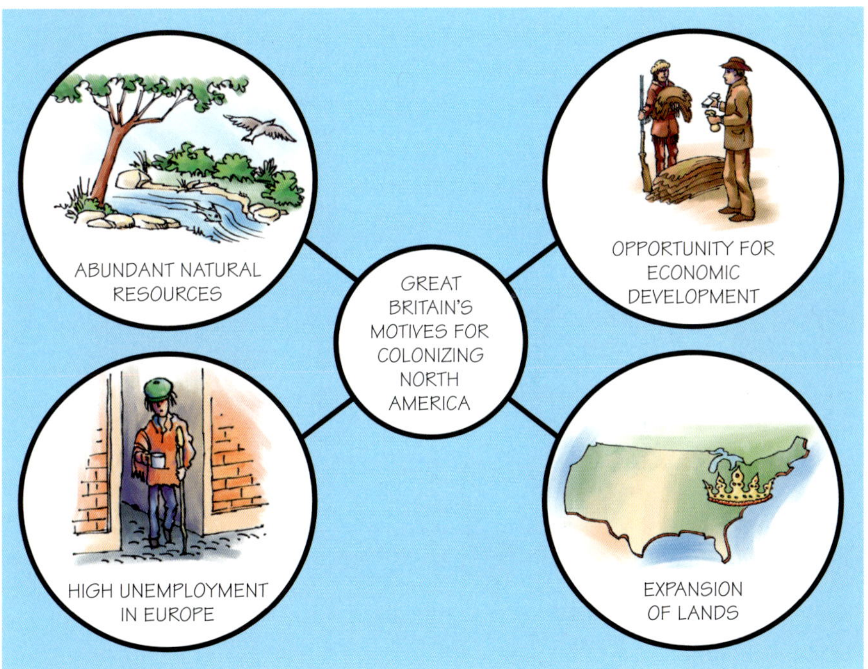

By using visual images and just a few words to describe the subject, you will be much better able to recall the information later.

Many students report that they remembered the drawings they drew on the mind map better than the descriptive words. Often, the drawing or doodle will help you recall the words and difficult concepts described in the diagram.

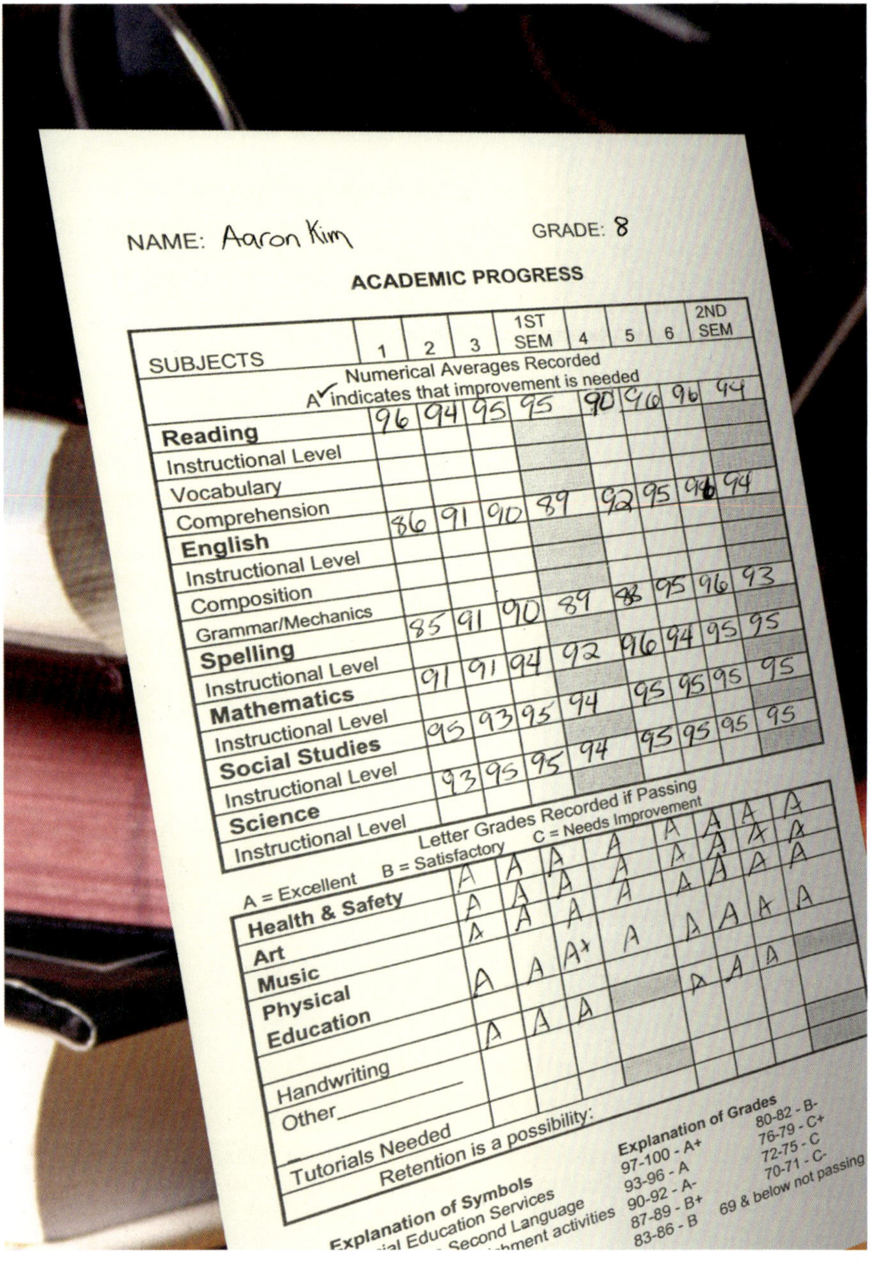

NAME: Aaron Kim GRADE: 8

ACADEMIC PROGRESS

SUBJECTS	1	2	3	1ST SEM	4	5	6	2ND SEM
Numerical Averages Recorded A✓ indicates that improvement is needed								
Reading	96	94	95	95	90	96	96	94
Instructional Level								
Vocabulary								
Comprehension								
English	86	91	90	89	92	95	96	94
Instructional Level								
Composition								
Grammar/Mechanics								
Spelling	85	91	90	89	88	95	96	93
Instructional Level								
Mathematics	91	91	94	92	96	94	95	95
Instructional Level								
Social Studies	95	93	95	94	95	95	95	95
Instructional Level								
Science	93	95	95	94	95	95	95	95
Instructional Level								

Letter Grades Recorded if Passing

A = Excellent B = Satisfactory C = Needs Improvement

	1	2	3	1ST SEM	4	5	6	2ND SEM
Health & Safety	A	A	A	A	A	A	A	A
Art	A	A	A+	A	A	A	A	A
Music	A	A	A		A	A	A	
Physical Education	A	A	A					
Handwriting								
Other ______								

Tutorials Needed

Retention is a possibility:

Explanation of Symbols

...ial Education Services

... Second Language

...hment activities

Explanation of Grades

97-100 - A+
93-96 - A
90-92 - A-
87-89 - B+
83-86 - B
80-82 - B-
76-79 - C+
72-75 - C
70-71 - C-
69 & below not passing

Improving Your Grades at School

For requirement 1, you must show that you earned an average grade of B or higher for one term, or that you have improved your grades over the previous term. What's the best way to go about doing this? Here is a simple step-by-step guide.

Organize Your Work Space

Find a place at home where you feel comfortable and where you can focus on the task at hand. The place you select should be well-lighted and relatively quiet at the time of day you will be doing your homework. It also should have a sturdy chair and a table or desk where you can spread out your papers and books.

Clean the area thoroughly before you start using it as your work space. Next, equip your space with college- or wide-ruled paper, some pens, a couple of pencils with good erasers, a small pencil sharpener, a ruler, a pair of scissors, a calculator, and a highlighter. These items, except for the paper, can be placed in a shoebox or other container if the area you use has multiple purposes and must be shared with family members. Place a dictionary, a thesaurus, and a wall or desk calendar within easy reach. Always put everything back in the same place.

Keep Your Work Space Organized

This ranks as its own category because it is the hardest thing for some students to do and yet it makes all the difference in the world. It should take less than three minutes to clean off your desk or table thoroughly after each session. Stack your papers in a neat pile, put your pens and materials back in the container, and place reference books back where they belong. Recycle any wastepaper immediately.

If you wonder why this is important, think about the impact of clutter and disorganization in your life. It can be overwhelming and time-consuming if you let clutter take over. Just finding things when they are buried under a pile of rubble can consume a lot of time better spent otherwise and can cause major frustration. Lighten your load: Clean up your space each time you use it.

Schedule Homework Time Each Day

Write down homework time on your calendar as a regular part of your schedule during weekdays. Many students prefer to do homework right after school so they can have their evenings free. But, if you participate in extracurricular activities right after school or if you focus better after dinner or early in the morning before school, choose the time that works best for you. Just remember that once you set your schedule it is up to you to keep it, so be realistic.

After you finish your homework, make a check mark on the calendar to indicate that you studied that day and completed your assignments. Be proud of each check mark you make: It means you achieved your academic goals for the day.

> If you are not assigned homework on a given day, use your homework time to organize your school papers and review your class notes, highlighting the important information you think you will need for tests.

Organize Schoolwork by Subject

Nothing accumulates faster in your school life than paperwork. If you are trying, like so many students, to stuff all your loose papers, assignment sheets, and homework into the tight plastic pocket of a three-ring binder, by the end of a semester, your binder will look like a bursting blob straight out of a horror film. Instead, tame the creepy beast. Group your papers by subject.

Count the number of subjects you are taking in school. Then, purchase different colored pocket folders or—if you expect a lot of paperwork—accordion folders for each subject area. Using a black marker, clearly label the front of the folders for each subject. Here's the trick: Bring these folders with you to class each day and use them to organize and store paperwork as you receive it.

When your teacher gives you homework, handouts, and other materials, immediately write the date on the top of each sheet. That way, you will know exactly when you received the information. Place the materials in chronological order inside the folder for that subject before you leave class. If you forget to bring your folder to school one day or don't have time to organize your work before the end of class, add the paperwork to the proper folder as soon as you get home.

With a busy schedule, you might sometimes find it necessary to study during the ride home from school, on the bus, or during lunch. That's OK. You might discover you can focus better with some background music, and that's OK, too.

Use a Pocket Organizer to Track Your Academic and Social Life

The pocket organizer, whether it is electronic or paper, should have large blank squares or a place for notes under each calendar day. Schedules change quickly, so if you are working on paper, use a pencil or an erasable pen to make notations.

First, write down when things are due or when tests are scheduled. But don't stop there. Jot down "Start studying for math test" a week before the test date, or "Pick up library books for science project" a month before you turn in your erupting volcano. Add social and extracurricular activities to your calendar, keeping in mind that your academic career is your most important responsibility and that your hobbies and social life should be balanced against that main duty.

Each week, transfer information from your pocket organizer or electronic notebook to your wall calendar so that you have a clear idea of how your schedule looks. Keep your pocket organizer with you each day at school and update it regularly.

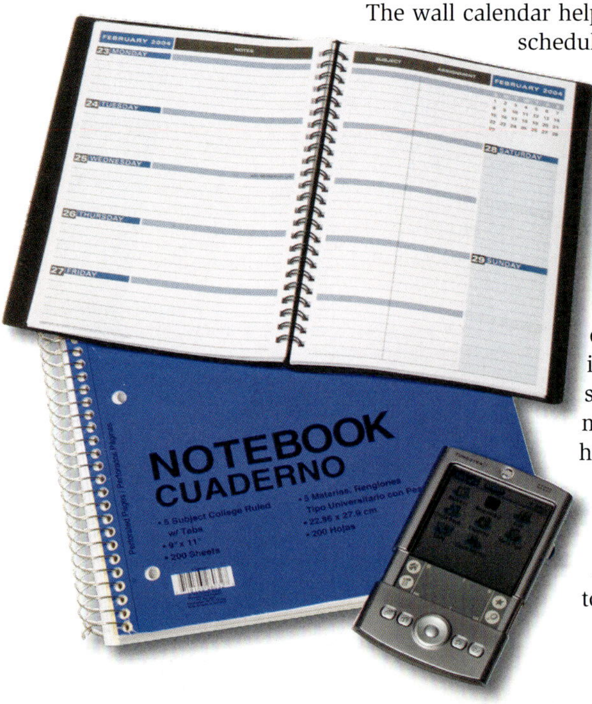

The wall calendar helps you follow your schedule when you are at home and apt to be thinking about other things. It also provides you with a backup calendar just in case you lose your pocket organizer.

Never underestimate the power of notes to jog your memory. If you have ever marveled at someone's incredible organizational skills, rest assured that most successful people rely heavily on notes to stay on track. This becomes crucial as you add more social activities and academic responsibilities to your schedule.

If you choose requirement 2c, take both your pocket organizer and your backup calendar with you to show your counselor how you organize your time and track your academic and social life.

What Kind of Student Are You?

Get out a piece of paper. Answer the following questions honestly about yourself. Remember, there are no wrong answers; this is just a guide to help you see yourself as you are right now in your role as a student.

1. "Where do I normally sit in a classroom?" (In the back, front, middle, or on the left or right side?)
2. "What is my normal posture at my desk?"
3. "Do I come to class prepared with my textbook, notebook, subject folder, pens, and pencils, or do I forget one or more of these items regularly?"
4. "Do I make direct eye contact with the teacher when he or she is lecturing?"
5. "Do I take notes in class? Can I read my own handwriting later and understand the general meaning of the topic?"
6. "Do I doodle or draw pictures in class? Do these pictures have anything to do with helping me remember the subject and information being presented?"
7. "Am I a good listener? Do I interrupt people when they speak, or do I listen quietly until they are finished and then reply?"
8. "Do I participate in classroom discussion and feel comfortable working in groups and on teams?"
9. "Do I pause to think before I speak, or do I frequently blurt out things without thinking first?"
10. "Do I like school and feel that it benefits me in many ways?"

Review your answers. For each question you answered in a negative way, now write down one positive thing you can do to change your mind about the way you think about that aspect of yourself as it relates to your education. For instance, if you answered question No. 2 with, "I slouch forward and rest my chin on my desk," your positive change could be to sit up straight and be more attentive.

If you teach yourself to think positively and present a can-do spirit in your learning and the way you interact with your peers and teachers, positive change will happen in your academic life.

Focusing on the negative aspects of your life can slow you down in the same way a parachute drags a race car to a halt. Positive thought creates positive momentum and positive action.

Learn Simple Test-Taking Strategies

When you prepare for tests, concentrate on one class at a time. Decide which information from your notes and textbooks will be important for you to learn for the test. Look at your courses and set your study priorities based on which subject requires more time to master. Always spend more time on tasks that you find difficult and do the tough ones first.

Texas State University's Student Learning Assistance Center offers students the following tips for preparing for tests. These tips are as important for elementary, junior high, and high school students as they are for young adults attending college.

If the test is a final, refer to earlier tests you have taken and browse the table of contents in your books to review the overall subject matter. Study your class notes, and read any unread material or reread anything you did not quite understand. Anticipate, as you are reading through the material, the types of questions that might be on the test. Think while you read. At the end of each page or section, test yourself to help you remember what you read.

Longer study periods are required to grasp broad concepts and to understand relationships between ideas. Underline, highlight, and summarize work, but do not spend your time recopying your notes. Recall important points about the various aspects of the course without looking at your notes or in the book. If your memory draws a blank, review that section again.

Math formulas, theories, definitions, and any complex terms that you must memorize require short but frequent practice sessions. As you review, test yourself at the end of each page or section to increase your retention.

Reading comprehension questions mainly involve reading a passage or short paragraph and then answering questions about it. Make sure you read correctly the test instructions and questions. You might find it helpful to read the questions before you read the passage. The questions may relate to the main theme or to general or detailed information within the reading material.

If you are at home and bored, work word puzzles, play chess or checkers, or play trivia and geography games. These fun side pursuits can help you improve your recall and strengthen your memory bank.

Daily physical exercise, even if it is only a brisk 15- to 20-minute walk, and taking brief study breaks will help your ability to concentrate and provide you with more energy to burn. It is fine to review material with others, but only after you have studied the subject matter on your own and feel confident that you know the material.

Use the Power of Positive Thinking

Train yourself to use the power of positive thought to improve your test performance. Repeat positive statements to yourself before taking tests. Tension and anxiety drain energy from your test performance, so tell yourself that you will do well.

Whenever you achieve a goal, acknowledge to yourself that you have succeeded. Give yourself a big pat on the back. Remember this: Goals do change over time. It is OK to change what you imagine to match changing goals.

To respond to an essay question on a test, begin with a strong sentence that clearly states your essay's main theme. Below that, follow up with key points that you plan to discuss. Expand upon your key points by writing a paragraph about each point.

Creative Visualization

Have you ever watched a downhill skier just before a final run in the Olympics? Standing atop a snow-covered mountain, the skier closes her eyes and seems to imagine the course in her head—every turn and bump, every patch of ice and pocket of deep powder—to her successful run to the bottom. Her hands move back and forth as if she is gripping ski poles. In the skier's mind, she is flying over the terrain faster than she's ever gone, effortlessly, to the roar of cheers at the finish line. This technique is called creative visualization. It is a simple technique that everyone can use.

Everyday, we use imagination without really thinking about it. Throughout the day, a running conversation plays inside our heads about other people, our own feelings, what we need to do from minute to minute, and what is happening around us. These words and ideas ultimately help shape and create our environment.

For instance, before an artist paints a painting, he feels inspired. In his head, he sees the painting or gathers some idea of what it will look like. Before an architect designs a house on paper, she mulls over the details in her mind. Before a basketball player makes a perfect three-pointer from downtown, he imagines the ball leaving his hands and hearing the sweet swish of the net.

Creative visualization can help you become aware of your thoughts and engage in positive statements about your life and what you do. The object is to set goals and go for what you want in life, using creative visualization to guide you toward your goals. The important thing is to use it to make positive change.

Energy tends to attract energy of a similar nature. When we create something, we always create it in thought form first. People consumed with negative thoughts tend to attract negative people. People with positive attitudes tend to attract people, situations, and events that match their positive expectations. You constantly create the conditions in which you live your life. Look at ways you might hold yourself back with negative feelings and beliefs. Only you can choose the best, most fulfilling life you can imagine.

How Your School Can Help You Get Better Grades

Public schools operate under the umbrella of a statewide academic curriculum that is passed by the legislature. This means that students in each state must meet specific education requirements, from passing courses to passing standardized tests, before they can graduate from high school. These educational requirements and the curriculum itself vary from state to state.

If you are struggling in a subject and need tutoring, your school might offer an after-school study program. Schools sometimes offer phone- or Internet-based tutoring. Give the tutor your undivided attention and don't be afraid to ask the person to repeat certain points that are unclear to you. Return to the study center as often as needed to become comfortable, knowledgeable, and confident about the subject.

If your parents are working with you to help you understand a subject better, ask your school if your state provides a study guide for your grade level and the subject in which you need help. For instance, if you are in the sixth grade and are having difficulty with math, request a grade six math study guide. In some states, study guides might be available online.

Study guides usually are written by teachers who have a great deal of experience in that particular subject. The guides are written in plain language so that parents and students can easily understand the requirements of a course and how to go about meeting them. Often, spending just a week working chapter by chapter through a study guide is enough to achieve an overall comprehension of the subject.

Standardized tests required by your state normally are released to the public every few years. Most states will publish the tests online so that students can use them to practice for the one they will be required to pass.

Check out your state education agency's student testing or student assessment division to see what resources and practice materials are available online.

Dr. Vicente Villa*

Until Dr. Vicente Villa retired from his teaching post in the spring of 2003, students could not hide from one of his 8 A.M. biology labs at Southwestern University (SU) in Georgetown, Texas. If students were absent, the professor phoned them at home to find out why they were not in class. Simply put, the man cares.

Dr. Vicente Villa, professor emeritus of biology and holder of the John H. Duncan Chair (retired 2003), was named U.S. Professor of the Year in 1993 by the Council for Advancement and Support of Education. Among other honors awarded with this title, he received a $10,000 cash prize from the Carnegie Foundation for the Advancement of Teaching.

He was chosen for the national award over 389 candidates from public and independent universities across the country. The decision to recognize Villa for his extraordinary commitment to teaching was based in large part on the strength of support from his current and former SU undergraduate students.

Part parent, part teacher, part pit bull with a strong appetite for science education, Dr. Villa is in a class all his own. Throughout his teaching career, he remained dedicated to his students' personal and professional welfare. His former students speak of him as though he belongs to them personally,

A Mexican American from Laredo, Texas, Villa worked as a shoe-shine boy on the banks of the Rio Grande River. Villa's father was one of the last of the Mexican vaqueros, or cowboys, who eked out a living along the U.S.-Mexico border. Villa's mother was legally blind. Neither of his parents had much of an education and both wanted their children to reach for a better future. They encouraged young Vicente to excel.

Villa says, "The bottom line is perseverance. Don't give up. Be a fighter. Those experiences really saved me." After he finished Laredo Junior College, Villa completed a B.S. in biology at the University of Texas at Austin and a Ph.D. in microbiology at Rice University.

When Villa arrived at Southwestern University in 1985, few of the university's Hispanic students majored in the sciences. He set out to change that and Villa worked with great energy to encourage science students to pursue medical, research, and teaching careers. In 1993, more than half of Villa's graduating students were admitted to the nation's top medical schools. Today, more than 10 percent of those graduating from SU with biology degrees are Hispanic.

An animated lecturer and deeply spiritual man, Villa exudes a passion for science. A colleague recalls watching Villa lecture, "Dr. Villa was waving his arms around wildly and moving fluidly—almost with the grace of a dancer, which is really remarkable when you consider that Vicente is not exactly a small man. Later on, I saw Vicente in the hall and asked him what he had been lecturing about so excitedly. He replied, 'When you lecture on the amoeba, you must imitate the amoeba!'"

Class after class, year after year, the following words rang in the ears of Villa's students: "Be a scholar! I urge you! Do the extra things that will make all this worthwhile!"

Now that he is retired, Villa plans to create an outreach program and perhaps a laboratory on wheels: "I want to bring a hands-on approach to science to children at a younger age. The way we are teaching science at this level is not turning kids on. I think we can do better."

*Portions reprinted with permission from Shannon Lowry, "Villa Named U.S. Professor of the Year," Southwestern Magazine, fall 1993; and D. Ann Shiffler, "Mr. Homecoming," Southwestern Magazine, 2002.

The Evacuation of Boston
PROSPECT HILL
"The Tories were thunder-struck, and
dejected. All was hurry and confusion: the
soldiers working . . . night and day, getti
board what [ships] they could as fast as
On the 17th of March in the morning they
evacuated the town."
Reverend William Gordon, April 6, 1776

Intellectual Curiosity: Your Passport to the World

Be proud of your brainpower and where it can take you. Seek personal enrichment through your discovery of interesting people, places, and things. Friendships bloom, doors open, and new pathways and adventures become possible when you actively seek out and explore your interests with a curious mind and an open heart.

Libraries, museums, state archives, historical societies, art galleries, amateur and professional theater productions, music venues, free lecture series, book clubs, outdoor events, wildlife exhibits, zoos, folk festivals, and state fairs are just some of the places where you can acquire a self-education. The list is endless. Get out there and teach yourself what you want to know!

If you choose requirement 2a, you will write a brief but concise one-page report on what you learned at the place you chose for self-education. Take a notepad, two pens or pencils, and perhaps a pen light with you. When you get there, take notes and record your impressions.

When you return home, immediately rewrite your notes into a one-page report. In your first paragraph, describe where

What fuels your imagination or piques your curiosity? What challenges and inspires you? When you research or participate in something that is of great interest to you, you are reaching for your own bright star.

Find out about free events in your area by reading the calendar section of your local newspaper and browsing local cultural sites online. Record dates and upcoming events on your calendar, then check with your parents in advance about making arrangements.

If you attend a concert, presentation, or other performance in a dimly lit theater, a pen light will allow you to see your notepad without disturbing others around you.

you went and why that particular place interested you. In the next two to three paragraphs, report what you saw and felt, any new or surprising information that you learned, and your overall impressions.

Should you choose requirement 2b, you will need to get your counselor's and parents' approval before you interview the two professionals who have challenging and rewarding careers. Phone interviews often are much easier to arrange when you are dealing with busy people. Just remember to have a notepad, a couple of pens or pencils, your calendar, and the questions you want to ask in front of you before you make the call.

First, identify two professional people you or your parents know (not your teachers or other school personnel) whom you admire or respect. This could be the owner of a small business, a doctor, nurse, plumber, architect, builder, electrician, computer programmer, journalist, political activist, photographer, or anyone with a career you would like to learn more about.

Next, write down five questions you would like to ask each person you plan to interview. Here are some examples.

- Where did you receive the education or training you needed to do this work?
- How did your education and training prepare you for your career?
- What do you find most rewarding about your profession?
- What is the most challenging or difficult aspect of your position?
- What types of events or activities do you participate in to help you continue to educate yourself in the subjects that interest you?

Third, contact the two people by phone. (Remember to have your questions, your calendar, a notebook, and two pens or pencils in front of you.) State your name clearly and the reason you are calling: "Hi, Mr. Martin. My name is Bob Barton. I'm working on the requirements for the Scholarship merit badge in Boy Scouts. I've been asked to interview two professional people who have careers I'm interested in learning more about. Would it be possible to arrange a time when I could do a brief phone interview with you to talk about your profession and how you got where you are today?"

If the person responds yes, politely ask him or her to suggest a specific time for you to call back. Confirm the time and date of the interview by repeating it back to the person. Immediately write down the interview time and the person's name and phone number on your calendar. Then, thank the person in advance for taking the time to talk to you and say goodbye. Don't forget to follow through and call for the interview at the exact time you promised.

The most important thing to remember as you interview someone is to be a good listener.

Often, when you approach a person about conducting a brief phone interview, he or she will agree to do it at that instant. That is why it is a good idea to have your questions written out and ready to ask. If the person says, "Sure, go ahead. Shoot," say thanks and then ask your questions one at a time. Be careful to write down only the gist of what the person says in response and not every single word that is said.

Once you finish the phone interview, review your notes quickly and make sure you have everything you need. If you want to ask a follow-up question that occurred to you during the interview, this is the time to do so. Ask the person if you can call again in case you have forgotten something important or want to confirm something that was said. Lastly, thank the person generously for taking the time and for helping you with your merit badge requirement. Then say goodbye.

Immediately rewrite your interview notes into a brief, one-page report that details the person's responses to your five questions. Review your report a few times before presenting it to your counselor. Then you will be prepared to paraphrase without reading your notes aloud.

Reading classics is a wonderful opportunity to see how people in the past viewed many of the same issues that concern us today.

The Classics Will Come Back to Haunt You—In a Good Way

Before you graduate from high school, you will be required to read a few classics. Reading classics can be challenging because the language often is different or more complex than the language we use today. However, reading classics is highly rewarding. Not only will you improve your vocabulary, but you also will learn the sources of some of the most important ideas in human history.

Classic literature includes those literary works widely read throughout history and valued for their influence on culture and society. Classic works span the centuries, from Greek and Roman literature to modern day. These works explore many of the same themes that are important to us today, only they do so from the perspective of the period in which they were written. The more you read, the broader your perspective on current events will be, and the better able you will be to think critically about the impact of current events on you and your community.

Likewise, reading classic literature is an opportunity to delve into the richness of language and the similarities and differences of people's experiences over time. You also can observe the common features of storytelling and how the features of storytelling have stayed the same or changed through the ages.

Ask your school or local librarian for a list of classic literature and devour great books like potato chips. As you read, think about the main idea of the book and its underlying themes and social commentary. Is the subject or general theme of the book similar to the themes of other books you have read in the past? Common themes include hope, courage, redemption, human failing, love and loss, discipline, and sacrifice. How is the author's writing influenced by the era in which he or she lived? Also watch for literary devices that shape the story, such as "flat" characters who only appear in a single scene to move the plot along and "round" characters whom you get to know intimately and are elaborated upon throughout the book.

Treasure Island, Huckleberry Finn, Moby Dick, The Hobbit, A Tale of Two Cities, Walden, The Grapes of Wrath, The Sun Also Rises, Jane Eyre, All Quiet on the Western Front, The Odyssey, Pride and Prejudice, The Great Gatsby, Uncle Tom's Cabin, A Separate Peace—these are books you might be assigned to read before you graduate from high school. The more classic literature you have read in your youth, the more valuable and well-rounded your overall education becomes in adulthood.

Mark Twain used humor and satire to comment on important issues in American society, such as slavery. His well-regarded novels include *Tom Sawyer, The Adventures of Huckleberry Finn,* and *A Connecticut Yankee in King Arthur's Court.*

If you have a hard time reading or if you read slowly, try classic books that have been turned into graphic novels. Pictures are worth a thousand words and improve remembering. Likewise, sometimes the themes explored in classics are difficult to understand. Study guides, such as *Sparknotes* and *Monarch Notes* are available for most classics. Study guides are particularly helpful if you are reading a classic book on your own and want to better understand its plot and themes.

Study guides like these can enhance your understanding of classic books such as *The Great Gatsby*.

DICTIONARY
KNOX TRAIL COUNCIL
BSA
MASSACHUSETTS
51

Methods of Research

If you choose requirement 2d, you will need to discuss with your counselor the advantages and disadvantages of the different methods of research available to you for school assignments, such as the library, books and periodicals, and the Internet.

A trained librarian can help you find resources you did not know existed. A librarian knows how to cross-reference your subject under different but related terms to find the maximum number of resources for you to use.

Libraries

Public libraries were, are, and always will be an important primary research tool for students, teachers, and people who do research as a profession. Your public library not only gives you free access to books, periodicals, and the Internet, but it also gives you access to reference librarians.

Rare or out-of-print books and reference books usually are not available for lending. If that is the case, you will have to read them at the library.

If the book or periodical you need is not available at your local library, you can request an interlibrary loan. Your librarian will request the book from the nearest public library that has the book. When the book arrives at your local library, you can check it out. The retrieval process usually takes no more than 10 days. Your librarian can tell you more about this service.

Books and Periodicals

Books are excellent resources for learning about historical events. Remember to look for different perspectives by reading books on the same subject written by authors with different points of view. For instance, if you were researching Custer's last stand at the Battle of Little Bighorn, you might read the personal papers of General Custer and rent a documentary on the battle to get an overview of what happened. But, you also might want to read *Black Elk Speaks,* a biography of Crazy Horse written by Nicholas Black Elk, to get the perspective of the Sioux and Cheyenne warriors who fought in that battle.

If you are researching a current event, look for information about it in periodicals such as magazines and newspapers. Remember to read more than one source to get different perspectives on the subject.

The *Reader's Guide to Periodical Literature* is the ultimate research tool at the library. No matter what topic you research, someone has published a research paper, or magazine or newspaper article about it. In larger research libraries, periodical literature has been stored on microfilm and is available for you to read. Ask your librarian to show you how to access these materials.

Whenever you refer to a book, magazine, CD, newspaper, or other published source in a report or project, be sure to give proper credit to the author and publisher. It is OK to use brief quotes from published sources as long as you properly credit your source by including the author's name, date of publication, article title, publication title, publisher, and page numbers in a footnote or resource section. Use direct quotes sparingly, however. Most of the time, you should record information by taking notes in your own words as you read through the research materials. Use these notes to create your report or project.

For examples of what citations look like, see the resources section at the back of this merit badge pamphlet.

Your public library also is a good place to check and recheck your facts. If you are unsure about any factual information, try to find three independent, reputable sources that will confirm your material. Write down the names of the articles or books where you found the information, the name of the publisher, the year it was published and the city in which it was published. Also, write down the page number on which you found the information. If a teacher questions your research, you can readily refer to the specific citation and back it up with other published sources.

Unfortunately, libraries often have limited hours and are not always open when you need to find something fast. If you live in a small town or even a big town with a small budget, your public library might not have the materials you need without requesting them through interlibrary loan. You might not have time to wait for materials to arrive from elsewhere. That's when the Internet can help.

The Internet

The Internet is a grand resource for academic research. Its biggest advantage is that it is fast, and it is available 24 hours a day, seven days a week, 365 days a year. Plus, the self-education you can get on the Internet is almost limitless. A click of your mouse will get you to a good search engine (see the resources section at the end of this pamphlet) where you can search by subject area, title, author, historical period, location, event, important names, organization names, or key phrases. Most websites also have a built-in search feature.

For example, a costume designer can access costume collections and museums online to find the perfect period clothing for a historic play set in 18th century India. What used to take days and weeks to research can now take only a few hours.

By the same token, a doctor working in a remote part of the world can connect to the Internet via satellite to get information on medical treatments. The Internet has radically changed the way we obtain information.

However, be aware that much of the information available on the Internet is incorrect. Anyone can post information on the Internet. Sometimes people post false information intentionally, but most of the time people pass along incorrect information without knowing it.

When researching on the Internet, it is particularly important to only rely on professional, reputable sources of information, no matter how trivial the information might be. Let's say you want to look up an NBA score from last night's game. You could check the Associated Press (AP), an established, respected newspaper wire service, or you could visit the official NBA website.

If you need up-to-the-minute information on breaking news, AP, Reuters, the New York Times, CNN, the British Broadcasting Corporation (BBC), and hundreds of other credible news sources are instantly available on the Internet. However, even news organizations have accidentally spread inaccurate information. If the story is still developing, check several news sources and use your critical reading skills to make sure you are getting the most accurate information.

Make sure to read news sources carefully to help determine what is fact, opinion, and interpretation. Information often can look or sound very similar, and it can be easy to mistake an opinion for fact.

The great advantage to using the Internet is that you have the entire world at your fingertips. Anything and everything is mentioned online. Just remember to click on your own good judgment before you log on, and to get your parent's permission first.

Tips for Online Safety

On the Internet, you can learn all sorts of things, click your way to a wide world of instant information, and even read whole books. Along with the convenience, though, comes some risk. When you are online, you need to be careful to guard your privacy and protect yourself from potentially harmful situations.

These tips will help you stay safe. Your parent, counselor, or librarian may talk with you about other rules for Internet safety. When you are at a library, you may also ask a librarian for a copy of that particular library's Internet rules.

1. Follow your family's rules for going online. Respect any limits on how long and how often you are allowed to be online and what sites you can visit. Do not visit areas that are off-limits. Just as there are places you don't go to in real life, there are places to avoid on the Internet.
2. Protect your privacy. Never exchange emails or give out personal information such as your phone number, your address, your last name, where you go to school, or where your parents work, without first asking your parent's permission. Do not send anyone your picture or any photographs unless you have your parent's permission.
3. Do not open emails or files you receive from people you don't know or trust. If you get something suspicious, trash it just as you would any other junk mail.
4. If you receive or discover any information that makes you uncomfortable, leave it and tell your parent. Do not respond to any message that is disturbing or hurtful.
5. Never agree to get together with someone you "meet" online, unless your parent approves of the meeting and goes with you.
6. Never share your Internet password with anyone (even if they sound "official") other than your parents or other responsible adults in your family.
7. Never shop online unless you have your parent's permission to do so.
8. Do not believe everything you see or read online. Along with lots of great information, the Internet has lots of junk. Learn to separate the useful from the worthless. Talk with your counselor or other experienced Web user about ways to tell the difference.
9. Be a good online citizen. Do not do anything that harms others or is against the law.

Scholarship and You

The positive approach you take and the activities you choose all will help you develop into a well-rounded and versatile individual.

The opportunities you discover as you earn the Scholarship merit badge may surprise you. You might find you have a special talent, hidden until now.

Leadership, Service, and Behavior

To fulfill requirement 3, you must get a note from the principal of your school that states that during the past year your behavior, leadership, and service have been satisfactory. Before you meet with your principal and request the note, carefully consider your strengths and successes as a student.

Have you been involved in a school play, choir, the band, tutoring or mentorship of younger students, athletics, an academic honor society, the school yearbook staff, debate club, a science fair, or any project or activity where you have used leadership or teamwork skills? When have you been most proud of your involvement and behavior in school? Write down everything you can think of that shows you are a well-rounded student who respects others and is self-motivated to succeed.

Using a couple of index cards, write down at least four short statements that detail your positive, active involvement in school this past year. Bring these index cards to your appointment and refer to them when you describe your achievements.

Contact your school secretary to make an appointment to see your principal. Politely tell the school secretary that you are completing a Boy Scout merit badge on scholarship and that you need a note from your school principal confirming that your behavior, leadership, and service have been satisfactory in the past year. Explain that you know the principal is busy and that the meeting should take no more than five minutes. Add that you will bring a prepared note that the principal can sign if he or she agrees that your skills have been satisfactory. Finally, thank the person who schedules the appointment for you.

Before the appointment, practice the points you want to make about your performance. Rehearse your informal speech several times in front of a mirror. Be honest, confident, and upbeat in your appraisal of yourself, but avoid boasting.

Type a brief note and print it in memo form. You can use the model below to craft your own note.

DATE: April 22, 2012

TO: Mr. John Jayson, Scoutmaster, BSA Troop 11

FROM: Mrs. Andrea Radcliff, Principal, Prairie Junior High School

RE: Student William Kossen's performance, 2011–2012 school year

I have met with student William Kossen to review his academic progress during this school year and I attest that his behavior, leadership, and service have been satisfactory.

Sincerely,

Mrs. Andrea Radcliff, Principal
Prairie Junior High School

Dress neatly for your appointment, and arrive on time. Have the note ready for the principal to sign and your index cards handy. State the reason for your visit. "As part of the requirements for my Boy Scout merit badge in scholarship, I need a signed note from you stating that my behavior, leadership, and service in school have been satisfactory this past year."

You might begin by saying something like the following: "During the past year, I brought my grades up to Bs by paying better attention in class and taking better notes. I've been involved in class projects in both history and English that have required teamwork and academic leadership skills. I have learned to manage my time effectively by using a pocket organizer and turning in my homework on time. In addition to balancing school with my extracurricular activities, such as Scouting and basketball practice, this past semester I tutored my next-door neighbor, who is having a hard time in math."

When you meet with your principal or other school official, make eye contact, smile widely, and shake hands. This creates an instant impression that you are confident, comfortable, and mature.

Then, simply state the bulleted information on your index cards, being careful to look up from your notes and make eye contact with your principal in a friendly manner at least a few times during your presentation.

In conclusion, politely ask your principal to sign the note you have prepared. Indicate that the note will only be used to show your merit badge counselor that you have fulfilled the merit badge requirement. After the principal signs your note, make eye contact, smile broadly, and shake hands as you say thank you. Then, leave quietly, with your signed note and index cards in hand. If the principal would like more time to review your academic records, leave the note with the principal and politely ask when you can return to pick it up. Remember your best etiquette whenever you are dealing with an older person in a position of authority.

Teamwork, School Projects, and Extracurricular Activities

If you choose requirement 4a, you will discuss with your counselor the benefits of your participation in an extracurricular school activity and what you have learned about the importance of teamwork.

If you have been a Scout for any length of time, you already have learned a great deal about the importance of teamwork. Campfires do not get built, meals do not get cooked, cleanup does not happen, and campfire programs do not get created or presented without plenty of teamwork on troop and patrol outings. When everyone pitches in and lends positive thoughts and action to a team effort, it is amazing how quickly and efficiently things get done. The more your troop works together, the more well-oiled the teamwork machine becomes.

The ability to work well with others is one of the most important skills you can bring to work, friendships, school, society, and life. The more brainpower and perspectives a group can devote to a problem or challenge, the better the overall results will be. Being part of a team involves keeping on task, speaking and acting positively, trusting your team members, working closely with people from varying backgrounds, and believing that the decisions reached by the group are stronger than those made by one person.

Think about the extracurricular activities in which you participate. How have you benefited from joining a group activity or organization? Write down all of the activities in which you participate, and include two or three positive benefits you have gained from your participation in each.

For instance, let's say you play on the school baseball team. Since joining the team, your batting average has improved a little, and your overall hand-eye coordination and body strength has increased with daily workouts. In addition, not only have you learned the joy of winning and the benefits of team play, but you also have learned how to perform well under pressure. When your team lost, you learned how to be a good sport by letting go of disappointment, resolving to do better next time, and shaking hands and congratulating the opposing team.

Teamwork requires patience, the ability to compromise and lead by example, and good listening and speaking skills. It requires follow-through to ensure that group ideas lead to successful results.

Now, write down at least two or three reasons why teamwork is important to the success of your extracurricular activities. Think about your attitude toward others on the team. Are you able to work well with people, even those you don't particularly like or those outside of your social group? Do you respect what others have to say? Under what circumstances are you able to compromise for the good of the group? Do you listen to the opinions of other people? Do you do your best to encourage other team members to participate in positive ways? Do you believe in a decision-making process that gives each person in the group an opportunity to contribute to the team's goals? Think about it. You couldn't play baseball by yourself. You need a pitcher, a batter, a catcher, and other players in the infield and outfield. You need a coach.

What do the other team members bring to the table? How can your group highlight an individual's personal strengths and play down his or her weaknesses? Are there team members who don't participate because they are afraid of making a mistake or failing? What positive, welcoming signs can you give to help people feel more secure in the group and more capable of contributing ideas without fear of rejection? How have you encouraged team members to share their best ideas? Do you readily include everyone in plans and decision making? Or, are you a member of a clique within a group, excluding certain team members or frequently putting down their ideas and input? Do you judge others too quickly or hold grudges against those who make mistakes?

If you are completing requirement 4a, write down four short sentences that detail the benefits you have gained from participating in an extracurricular activity.

Next, think about the importance of teamwork in that extracurricular activity. You might remember a small incident that was best resolved by team members working together or a larger project that required everyone's best efforts to make it successful. Perhaps you went to a team member who was stronger than you are in a specific skill and asked for help to improve your own performance and that of the team. Or, you might have been the one who helped a teammate with some part of the work that was particularly difficult. Your team may have learned more from its mistakes this year than from its successes. Explain how your team's setbacks helped the team work better together.

If you choose requirement 4b, discuss with your counselor your participation in a school project during the past semester where you were part of a team. Write down the specific positive contributions you made to the team and the project. Explain how you contributed to the project's success.

Think of contributions to the project made by other team members that you particularly appreciated. How did the group's attitude affect your team overall? Discuss what you learned that will help make you a better team member in the future.

Life After High School

A solid high school education will give you a good start with learning how to think and make good decisions. After graduation you can put your skills to work at college or perhaps pursue a career that requires technical knowledge or utilizes your artistic talents.

Prepare for College While You Are in High School

In your freshman year of high school, start talking to your school counselor, teachers, friends, and parents about college. Find out where they went, what courses they took, what activities they did, and what campus social life was like.

Purchase or borrow from the library a college directory that features detailed descriptions of universities and colleges. College directories also are available on the Internet. Make sure to visit the websites of specific colleges you want to learn more about.

Research scholarships and grants in your junior year (numerous reference guides can be found in your library) and record on your calendar the deadlines by which you must apply during your senior year.

If your family takes a vacation between your freshman and sophomore year and you are traveling near colleges you would like to visit, ask if you can take a side trip to see them. Make an appointment with the college admissions office in advance so you and your parents can receive a private or group tour.

If you don't know what subject area you would like to pursue as your major, consider the courses you particularly like in high school. Your school counselor's office might offer career assessment tests that will help you match your skills to a career. Look up colleges that have strong academic programs in the fields you might want to pursue.

Then check out the campus environment. Where will you be comfortable for at least four years? Do you like rural or urban settings? What kind of climate do you enjoy? Do you want to attend a big school with a large student body or a small school with limited class sizes? Check out the teacher-to-student ratio in your reference guide.

You also should consider the kind of social life you lead, your hobbies, and the kinds of activities the college offers. If you like coffeehouses, movies, and live theater, you probably will not want to attend a rural school where the featured activities are backpacking and mountain climbing. By the same token, if you like peaceful country living, you might not enjoy going to college in the heart of New York City.

Write to the colleges in which you are interested. Ask for a packet of information about the school. Visit the colleges long enough to poke around campus, sit in on a class, and look at the residence halls. Eat at the campus cafeteria and do not be afraid to ask current students what the college is like and what they like or dislike about it. Feel out and observe every aspect of campus life that you can.

Narrow down the choices by the end of your junior year in high school. Look at the college application form for each of the schools to which you want to apply. Get a clear idea of each school's admission requirements. You will begin applying to colleges in your senior year, but by then, you will have a tremendous advantage because of the knowledge you gained by starting the process early.

Along with your application form, you likely will have to submit a 500-word essay on a topic of the college's choice. You may be asked to write an essay about your own life, someone you admire, a memorable experience, or a political or social issue. Some colleges also require you to answer a few open-ended questions about your decision to apply or your favorite book or hobby and what you enjoy about it most.

Application forms do not vary much between colleges or from year to year. The form you fill out will ask a fairly standard set of questions about your test scores, education, extracurricular activities, and family background.

Standardized exit-level high school tests and college entrance test scores, along with a high school transcript that shows your grades and overall grade point average, also will be required. Usually, colleges require that you take the ACT Assessment and three SAT II Subject Tests or the SAT I Reasoning Test. You can't go wrong taking the International Baccalaureate (IB) or Advanced Placement (AP) tests as well.

In your sophomore or junior year, you will take the PSAT, a practice test to prepare you for the SAT I. But, do not be fooled into thinking that the PSAT does not matter. The score from your junior year PSAT is used to determine whether you will qualify for scholarships and grants, including the National Merit Scholarships. These come with a cash prize that will help you cut the cost of your college tuition. Study for the PSAT by purchasing a PSAT study guide, reading through it several times, and taking some practice tests. This will help you become comfortable with the types of questions these tests ask.

Colleges also look at how well-rounded your skills are. This is where extracurricular activities become important. Get involved in things that interest you. If you like writing, join the student newspaper or yearbook staff. If you like sports, try out for the team of your choice. There is no magic number of activities you need to be involved in to secure the interest of a college, so pursue hobbies and activities that are interesting to you. Remember to keep a record of what you do and of any awards or special recognitions you receive. It is easy to forget information as you move through high school and college, so keep a list and store it in a safe place.

Foster good relationships with your teachers, counselors, and employers. You will need evaluations or recommendations from various people to get into a good college, so start developing those relationships now. Raise your hand in class—ask questions. Volunteer to do extra tasks for your teachers or employer. Ask your counselors for help with college planning. Seek guidance and advice from people in positions of authority whom you respect, and be open about your goals and interests with them so they know you are motivated and goal-oriented.

When the time comes to ask for a letter of recommendation, your employers, teachers, and counselors should know you pretty well and have glowing things to say about your character.

Education and Your Future

You are now heading down the home stretch toward your Scholarship merit badge.

If you choose requirement 5a, you will write a report of 250 to 300 words about how the education you receive in school will be of value to you in the future and how you will continue to educate yourself in the future. Even if you don't know what career you would like to pursue as an adult, consider as you write your report how your education in school will help you throughout life, regardless of the career you choose.

Begin your report by stating your enrolled grade, what school you attend, and how long you have attended that school. For instance, you might begin, "I am a seventh grade student at Rockland Junior High School. I moved to Rockland from Storyville last year and have just started to feel at home here."

Next, describe the classes you are taking currently and how what you are learning in each will help you in the future in some practical way. For instance, you might say, "I now take math, English literature, social studies, science, and art. Each of my classes teaches me skills I can use to learn and try new things."

Then, for each course you are taking, write a paragraph that describes the basic skills you are learning and how what you are learning can be applied in everyday life.

The last paragraph of your report should detail how you will continue to educate yourself in the future. This is where you can describe your specific areas of interest—academic or otherwise—and how you plan to learn more about them. For example, you might want to learn how to play guitar by taking group lessons and practicing in your room each day. Or, your goal might be to volunteer at a local theater in exchange for seeing performances for free. Your goal might be to join a running club and gradually work up to completing a half marathon.

Whatever you decide, use the last paragraph to describe how you plan to use education to better yourself and the quality of your life.

Should you choose requirement 5b to complete your merit badge requirements, you will write a report of 250 to 300 words about two careers that interest you. Your report should include how specific classes and good scholarship will help you achieve your career goals. Go to the library and research educational or technical training needed to pursue these careers. Ask a reference librarian to show you where the latest college guides are, then check to see which colleges and universities in the United States provide that training.

Research and write down the type of education you will need to obtain a position in the fields of your choice. Then, write down the colleges or technical institutes where you can receive training in those fields. Check college guides (see the resources section at the back of this book) to find out about the entrance requirements of the universities or training institutes you have selected.

Colleges sometimes will publish a list of recommended subjects that high school students should take to prepare for college study. See if you can find out which classes will best prepare you for college. If you have a hard time finding this information, ask your school counselor for help.

Scholarships, which can dramatically reduce the cost of your college education, are available for nearly every professional pursuit. Find out about the scholarships available to people who want to enter the fields you have selected. Also, check to see what types of scholarships and grants are available from the college you would like to attend, and find out what is required to apply.

Browse reference books on scholarships to find out about general scholarships for which you might be eligible. For instance, the Boy Scouts of America has a scholarship program for Scouts. Or, if any member of your family or ancestors have ever served in the U.S. military, you can apply for one of several

American Legion scholarships. Many of these scholarships require you to write a patriotic essay on a theme picked by the organization offering the scholarship. Other scholarships are available for students who obedience train a dog or who contribute a winning recipe to a contest. Federal grants, such as the Pell grant, are available to students whose families have financial need. Students can apply for these federal funds and the grants are awarded based on the family's income.

Now that you have a clear idea of the education you will need to pursue the two careers you have chosen, research the career opportunities in those fields. You might interview someone working in the profession to get an idea of the classes that are particularly helpful to take and the type of work or internships that will help you get experience in that field.

You can write a 250- to 300-word report on both careers, or a 125- to 150-word report on each career. Just remember to elaborate on how good scholarship in general will help you achieve your career goals.

Scholarship Resources

Scouting Resources

Boy Scout Journal; Personal Management, Public Speaking, and *Reading* merit badge pamphlets; also see merit badge pamphlets on particular careers or vocations.

Visit the Boy Scouts of America's official retail website at http://www.scoutstuff.org for a complete listing of all merit badge pamphlets and other helpful Scouting materials and supplies.

Books

Cottrell, Stella. *The Study Skills Handbook.* Palgrave Macmillan, 2003.

Nourse, Kenneth A. *How to Write Your College Application Essay,* 2nd ed. McGraw-Hill, 2001.

Kaplan, Ben. *The Scholarship Scouting Report: An Insider's Guide to America's Best Scholarships.* HarperResource, 2003.

Morgenstern, Julie and Jessi Morgenstern-Colon. *Organizing From the Inside Out for Teenagers.* Owl Books, 2002.

Tanabe, Gen S., and Kelly Y. Tanabe. *Accepted! 50 Successful College Admission Essays,* 2nd ed. SuperCollege, 2005.

———. *Get Into Any College: Secrets of Harvard Students,* 5th ed. SuperCollege, 2006.

VonGruben, Jill F. *College Countdown: The Parent's and Student's Survival Kit for the College Admissions Process.* McGraw-Hill, 1999.

Wise, Jessie and Susan Wise Bauer. *The Well-Trained Mind: A Guide to Classical Education at Home,* rev. ed. Norton and Company, 2004.

Organizations and Websites

Federal Student Aid

U.S. Department of Education
Website: http://studentaid.ed.gov

This government website provides complete information on FSA programs, including how to prepare for and choose schools, apply for funding, and repay student loans.

Google

Website: http://www.google.com

Use this search engine to comb the Internet on any subject using key words and phrases.

National Endowment for Financial Education

Website: http://www.nefe.org

This organization is "dedicated to improving the financial well-being of all Americans." Its website is a tremendous resource for college-bound students and anyone seeking information about funding a higher education.

SuperCollege.com

Website: http://www.supercollege.com

This helpful online resource for college applicants contains strategies and tips for exploring colleges, completing the application process, and finding and applying for scholarships.

Acknowledgments

The Boy Scouts of America is grateful to Carolyn Snowbarger, chief of staff of the Office of Elementary and Secondary Education at the U.S. Department of Education, and her staff for their assistance with this revised edition of the *Scholarship* merit badge pamphlet.

The Boy Scouts of America is grateful to the men and women serving on the Merit Badge Maintenance Task Force for the improvements made in updating this pamphlet.

Photo and Illustration Credits

Dynamic Graphics Inc., Vol. 59, Education, ©1999—page 22

HAAP Media Ltd., courtesy—cover *(microscope, laptop, calculator, university)*

©Jupiterimages.com—pages 6 and 16 *(background)*

The Mark Twain House and Museum, Hartford, Conn., courtesy—page 36

Library of Congress Prints and Photographs Division—page 9

©Photos.com—cover *(periodic table);* pages 34 and 53

Shutterstock.com—pages 26 (106120829 ©Andresr), 33 (76567660 ©.shock), 44 (47582029 ©Lasse Kristensen), 46 (50734651 ©bikeriderlondon), 50 (7525564 ©Yuri Arcurs), and 57 (71166679 ©Monkey Business Images), 2012 Used under license from Shutterstock.com

Southwestern University, Georgetown, Texas, courtesy—page 28

All other photos and illustrations not mentioned above are the property of or are protected by the Boy Scouts of America.

James Alexander—pages 4, 30, and 38

Dan Bryant—page 10

Darrell Byers—page 33

Daniel Giles—page 7

Vince Heptig—page 24

Doug Knutson—page 39

John McDearmon—all illustrations on pages 14–15

Frank McMahon—page 8

Brian Payne—pages 17, 27, 32, and 52

Randy Piland—pages 40 and 58